MANTIS SHRIMP VS. LIONFISH

BY KIERAN DOWNS

BELLWETHER MEDIA • MINNEAPOLIS, MN

™

Torque brims with excitement perfect for thrill-seekers of all kinds. Discover daring survival skills, explore uncharted worlds, and marvel at mighty engines and extreme sports. In *Torque* books, anything can happen. Are you ready?

This edition first published in 2023 by Bellwether Media, Inc.

No part of this publication may be reproduced in whole or in part without written permission of the publisher. For information regarding permission, write to Bellwether Media, Inc., Attention: Permissions Department, 6012 Blue Circle Drive, Minnetonka, MN 55343.

Library of Congress Cataloging-in-Publication Data

Names: Downs, Kieran, author.
Title: Mantis shrimp vs. lionfish / by Kieran Downs.
Other titles: Mantis shrimp versus lionfish
Description: Minneapolis, MN : Bellwether Media, 2023. | Series: Torque: animal battles | Includes bibliographical references and index. | Audience: Ages 7-12 | Audience: Grades 4-6 | Summary: "Amazing photography accompanies engaging information about mantis shrimp and lionfish. The combination of high-interest subject matter and light text is intended for students in grades 3 through 7"– Provided by publisher.
Identifiers: LCCN 2022001058 (print) | LCCN 2022001059 (ebook) | ISBN 9781644877616 (library binding) | ISBN 9781648348778 (paperback) | ISBN 9781648348075 (ebook)
Subjects: LCSH: Stomatopoda–Juvenile literature. | Pterois volitans–Juvenile literature.
Classification: LCC QL444.M375 D69 2023 (print) | LCC QL444.M375 (ebook) | DDC 595.3/796–dc23/eng/20220112
LC record available at https://lccn.loc.gov/2022001058
LC ebook record available at https://lccn.loc.gov/2022001059

Editor: Rebecca Sabelko   Designer: Josh Brink

Printed in the United States of America, North Mankato, MN.

TABLE OF CONTENTS

THE COMPETITORS 4

SECRET WEAPONS 10

ATTACK MOVES 16

READY, FIGHT! 20

GLOSSARY............................ 22

TO LEARN MORE 23

INDEX...................................... 24

THE COMPETITORS

Fierce battles between tough creatures take place in the ocean. Mantis shrimp pack a powerful punch. They are ready to fight.

Lionfish also have special weapons. Their sharp spines keep them safe during battles. Who would come out on top in a fight between these ocean **predators**?

There are more than 350 different **species** of mantis shrimp. They are named after praying mantises because of their similar front legs. Mantis shrimp mostly live along coasts around the world. But some can be found in deeper waters.

Mantis shrimp are often brightly colored. Their large eyes sit on stems that stick out from their heads.

ZEBRA MANTIS SHRIMP

ZEBRA MANTIS SHRIMP PROFILE

| 0 INCHES | 6 INCHES | 12 INCHES | 18 INCHES |

LENGTH
UP TO 15 INCHES
(38 CENTIMETERS)

WEIGHT
AROUND 3.2 OUNCES
(91 GRAMS)

HABITAT

CORAL REEFS

ZEBRA MANTIS SHRIMP RANGE

☐ RANGE

RED LIONFISH PROFILE

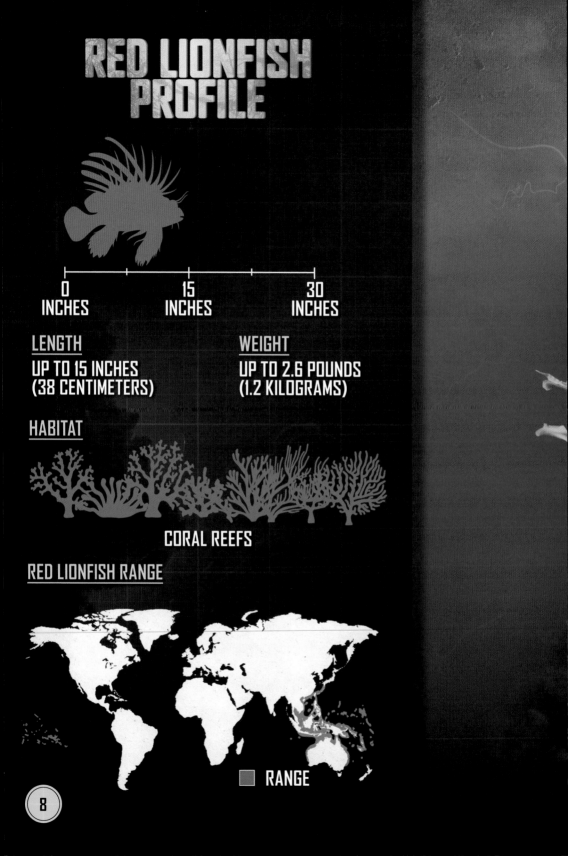

```
0          15         30
INCHES     INCHES     INCHES
```

LENGTH
UP TO 15 INCHES
(38 CENTIMETERS)

WEIGHT
UP TO 2.6 POUNDS
(1.2 KILOGRAMS)

HABITAT

CORAL REEFS

RED LIONFISH RANGE

■ RANGE

There are many different species of lionfish found in oceans around the world. They often have red or brown and white stripes. Around 18 spines stick out from their bodies. Their fins spread out like fans.

Many lionfish make their homes in **coral reefs** and rocky areas. These **carnivores** eat smaller fish and **mollusks**.

RED LIONFISH

A LOT OF EGGS

Female lionfish can lay about 2 million eggs per year!

SECRET WEAPONS

Mantis shrimp can move each eye independently. This helps the shrimp see all the way around themselves. Each eye can also see **depth**. This allows mantis shrimp to easily spot both **prey** and danger.

RED LIONFISH SPINE

UP TO 3.3 INCHES
(8.4 CENTIMETERS)

Lionfish use their spines to protect themselves. Each spine packs powerful **venom**. The fish stab their spines into enemies that try to attack.

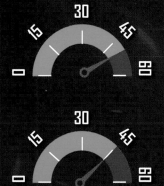

50 MILES (80 KILOMETERS) PER HOUR

PEACOCK MANTIS SHRIMP

45 MILES (72 KILOMETERS) PER HOUR

HUMAN

Mantis shrimps' front legs can **unfurl** at high speeds. This lets the shrimp deliver fast, powerful punches. Their punches are faster than the blink of a human eye!

Lionfish use their colors as **camouflage**.
They hide among colorful coral reefs.
This allows lionfish to sneak up on their prey.

MANTIS SHRIMP

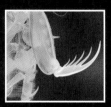

INDEPENDENTLY MOVING EYES

FAST PUNCHES

STRONG CLAWS

HAMMER-LIKE CLAW

Mantis shrimp claws differ by species. Some mantis shrimp have sharp, pointed claws. They stab their prey. Others smash their targets with hammer-like claws.

LIONFISH

VENOMOUS SPINES

CAMOUFLAGE

WIDE FINS

Lionfish have fins on the sides of their bodies. These fins can unfold to make the fish appear larger. They also use these fins to trap prey in corners.

ATTACK MOVES

BUBBLE BURST

Even if a mantis shrimp misses its punch, the bubble formed from it can still hurt enemies. Their punches are fast enough to boil the water around them!

Mantis shrimp use their punches to catch prey. Mantis shrimp with hammer-like claws can easily break shells. Then, they eat the animal inside the shell.

Lionfish are most active at night. They are **ambush hunters**. Lionfish wait for their prey while blending into their surroundings. Then, they attack!

SEEING COLOR

Mantis shrimp are able to see types of light that humans cannot. This lets mantis shrimp see many more colors than humans can see.

BURROW

Mantis shrimp are highly **territorial**. They stand at the openings of their **burrows**. They punch at any enemies that come near their homes.

Lionfish use their fins to trap prey. They unfold them to block their prey's escape. Then, lionfish snap at their prey. They swallow it whole!

READY, FIGHT!

A hungry lionfish is on the hunt. It spots a mantis shrimp and slowly approaches. The lionfish opens its fins and traps the mantis shrimp against rocks as it draws near.

The lionfish snaps at the mantis shrimp. But the mantis shrimp fires a deadly punch. Its claw smashes into the lionfish. The lionfish is defeated!

GLOSSARY

ambush hunters—animals that sit and wait to catch their prey

burrows—tunnels or holes in the ground used as animal homes

camouflage—colors and patterns used to help an animal hide in its surroundings

carnivores—animals that only eat meat

coral reefs—structures made of coral that usually grow in shallow seawater

depth—the distance from the front of something to the back as well as the top of something to the bottom

fierce—strong and intense

mollusks—animals that lack backbones and usually have shells

predators—animals that hunt other animals for food

prey—animals that are hunted by other animals for food

species—kinds of animals

territorial—ready to defend a home area

unfurl—to open or unroll

venom—a poison made by lionfish

TO LEARN MORE

AT THE LIBRARY

Drimmer, Stephanie Warren. *Animal Showdown: Round Two: Surprising Animal Matchups with Surprising Results.* Washington, D.C.: National Geographic, 2019.

Gunasekara, Mignonne. *Clever Creatures.* Minneapolis, Minn.: Bearport Publishing Company, 2021.

Murray, Julie. *Lionfish.* Minneapolis, Minn.: Abdo, 2020.

ON THE WEB

FACTSURFER

Factsurfer.com gives you a safe, fun way to find more information.

1. Go to www.factsurfer.com

2. Enter "mantis shrimp vs. lionfish" into the search box and click 🔍.

3. Select your book cover to see a list of related content.

INDEX

ambush hunters, 17

attack, 11, 17

burrows, 18

camouflage, 13

carnivores, 9

claws, 14, 16, 21

colors, 6, 9, 13, 18

coral reefs, 9, 13

eggs, 9

eyes, 6, 10

fins, 9, 15, 19, 20

food, 9

habitat, 6, 7, 8, 9

hunt, 20

legs, 6, 12

night, 17

ocean, 4, 5, 9

predators, 5

prey, 10, 13, 14, 15, 16, 17, 19

punch, 4, 12, 16, 18, 21

range, 6, 7, 8, 9

size, 7, 8, 11, 15

species, 6, 9, 14

speeds, 12

spines, 5, 9, 11

territorial, 18

trap, 15, 19, 20

venom, 11

water, 6, 16

weapons, 5, 14, 15

The images in this book are reproduced through the courtesy of: Beverly Speed, front cover (mantis shrimp); Richard Whitcombe, front cover (lionfish), p. 20 (coral); Francesco_Ricciardi, p. 4; Laura Dts, p. 5; SeaTops/ Alamy, pp. 6-7, 14 (claw); Levent Konuk, pp. 8-9; Steve Jones/ Alamy, p. 10; Pelagija, p. 11; DiveSpin, p. 12; Aaronejbull87, p. 13; Alex Permiakov, p. 14 (eyes); Paul R. Sterry/ Alamy, p. 14 (fast punch); Blue Planet Archive CMA/ Alamy, p. 14; Vitaliy6447, p. 15; Mayumi.K.Photography, p. 15 (spines); Elena Yakimova, p. 15 (camouflage); Eitan Ben Zvi, p. 15 (fins); Daniela Dirscherl/ AGEFotoStock, p. 16; Norbert Probst/ Alamy, p. 17; Charles Bokman, p. 18; Rich Carey, p. 19; Arunee Rodloy, pp. 20-21 (lionfish); Gerald Robert Fischer, pp. 20-21 (mantis shrimp).